SARAH WINCHESTER: BEYOND THE MYSTERY

Researched by
Bennett Jacobstein

Edited by
Fran Galt

Sarah Winchester: Beyond the Mystery

Copyright © 2019

Published by Kindle Direct Publishing

Researcher: Bennett Jacobstein

Editor: Fran Galt

ISBN 978-1-79461-660-8

All rights reserved. No part of this work may be reproduced, scanned, or distributed in any printed or electronic form without permission. All information in this work was obtained from publicly available documents.

CONTENTS

Researcher's Note

Acknowledgments

Introduction

Chapter

1. Sarah in Connecticut
2. Sarah Builds Her Mansion
3. An Architectural Marvel
4. Sarah Builds Her Hospital
5. The Mansion after Sarah's Death
6. Misconceptions about the Mansion
7. The Kind and Generous Sarah
8. Letters to Jennie
9. Sarah's Legacy

Notes

Bibliography

RESEARCHER'S NOTE

All research material consulted for this publication was obtained from publicly-available sources. Newspaper and magazine articles were retrieved from public online sources or viewed in person at library collections. Archives in California and Connecticut provided an opportunity to view personal correspondence and other related material. Detailed information may be found in the Bibliography section of this book.

ACKNOWLEDGMENTS

We would like to thank Mary Jo Ignoffo for her pioneering research on Sarah Winchester. She is the author of *Captive of the Labyrinth: Sarah L Winchester, Heiress to the Rifle Fortune* (University of Missouri Press, 2010). We highly recommend this book for those interested in a full-length biography of Sarah Winchester.

Special acknowledgments:

to Catherine Mills and History San Jose

to the Interlibrary Loan department of the New York Public Library

to Susan Dee, archivist at the Yale New Haven Hospital, for fact checking the "Sarah Builds her Hospital" chapter

to Ellen Gilmore and Debbie Jacobstein for editing and proofreading

to N.E. for her assistance with research and helping us get our thoughts down on paper

INTRODUCTION

Sarah Winchester was a brilliant, creative and generous woman. She lost her only child, Annie, at six weeks old. Her beloved husband William, heir to the Winchester rifle fortune, died at a young age from tuberculosis. Sarah never recovered from her two heartbreaking losses. Yet through all her pain she was focused on helping those in need.

Sarah spent major parts of her adult life on two building projects. Both of them live on today, 97 years after her death.

In San Jose, California, Sarah built an architectural marvel, a mansion in the American Queen Anne revival style reflecting great beauty and great innovation. The mansion has operated since 1923 as a tourist attraction known as the Winchester Mystery House. The house is a California Historical Landmark and is on the National Register of Historic Places.

Throughout the years rumors have been associated with Sarah and her house. The rumors suggest that the grief-stricken widow sought comfort from a medium in Boston who told her she was being cursed by the spirits of those killed by the Winchester rifle. She should move west, the medium said, and build a house and never stop building. As long as construction continued, she was told, she would not die. The rooms would shelter the good spirits and the sound of hammers would drive away the bad spirits. These rumors led to Sarah being portrayed as eccentric and crazy.

In West Haven, Connecticut, Sarah funded the building and operation of a hospital for patients with tuberculosis. The hospital, honoring her husband, was named the William Wirt Winchester Annex for Tuberculosis. Sarah was especially concerned with helping those of limited economic means. Over the years thousands of lives have been saved through the work of this hospital. Although the hospital no longer exists, the fund Sarah created continues to support the Winchester Chest Clinic, now part of the Yale New Haven Hospital.

Sarah's hospital remains virtually unknown, whereas Sarah's mansion is toured by a steady stream of visitors from around the world. The mansion was the setting for the 2018 film *Winchester*, a paranormal thriller starring Academy-Award-winning actress Helen Mirren. The movie was advertised as "inspired by true events." It is true that Sarah and the house both existed, but that is where the "true" events end.

The rumors surrounding the house continue to be told. Historical research including newspaper and magazine articles, personal correspondence, and interviews with Sarah's contemporaries reveals an alternative explanation of Sarah Winchester and her mansion.

Sarah as a young woman. Courtesy, History San Jose.

CHAPTER 1

SARAH IN CONNECTICUT

Sarah Lockwood Pardee was born in New Haven, Connecticut, in either 1839 or 1840. No birth certificate has been located, and U.S. Census records have conflicting information. She was the fifth of seven children (six girls, one boy) born to Leonard Pardee and Sarah Burns Pardee. Their first child was also named Sarah, but passed away at the age of one. This second Sarah was given the nickname of Sallie, after her paternal grandmother, Sally Pardee Goodyear. Most of Sarah's relatives referred to Sarah as Sallie.[1]

Sarah's father, Leonard Pardee, was born in 1807 in Hamden, Connecticut, near New Haven. He came from a long line of woodworkers going back four generations. As a young man, Leonard used his woodworking skills to manufacture small parts needed by the many factories that had appeared as a result of the American Industrial Revolution.

Around 1850, Pardee established Leonard Pardee and Company as a mill and wood shop. The shop was located next to the Pardees' new home in an upper-middle-class section of New Haven. This afforded young Sarah, as she was growing up, an opportunity to observe woodworkers practicing their craft. Sarah's fascination with the wood arts lasted the rest of her life.

Sarah's middle name, Lockwood, was in recognition of her father's good friend, Lockwood Sanford. Sanford was a well-known engraver whose wood blocks were used in the illustration of many books and catalogs as well as decorative book plates. This connection added to Sarah's love of decorative woodwork.

Growing up in New Haven, Sarah was taught by private tutors through whom she learned to speak several languages. She also became a skilled musician on the piano, organ and violin. Sarah excelled in all of her studies, and also developed a lifelong appreciation of the works of Shakespeare.

When Sarah was between eleven and thirteen years of age, the Pardee home was on the same street as the Winchester home. The Winchesters were the founders of the Winchester Repeating Arms Company which became one of the best known gun manufacturers in American history. Sarah Pardee and William

William Winchester. Courtesy, History San Jose.

Winchester became childhood friends. In 1862 they were married.

Sarah and William's only child was born on June 15, 1866. The baby, named Annie Pardee, exhibited symptoms of digestive problems from birth. She failed to thrive. Dr. Ives, the family physician, gave a diagnosis of marasmus. Annie was not able to obtain nutrients from her food, and slowly starved to death. She died on July 25, 1866.

Sarah and William Winchester shared a home with William's parents where Sarah learned money-management skills from William's father, Oliver Winchester. She was able to utilize this skill later in her life. As the Winchester Repeating Arms Company became more successful, the family decided to build a new residence large enough to house them all. They hired well-known architect Henry Austin to design their new hilltop home in New Haven.

William and his father were busy working at the Winchester Repeating Arms Company, so Sarah served as the primary contact with the architect. Together, Henry Austin and Sarah designed a 20,000-square-foot mansion with marble floors, ornamental wood carvings, elaborate fireplaces and elegant chandeliers. The structure had a four-story campanile. Floor to ceiling windows allowed for a magnificent view of the surrounding area. Working with architect Henry Austin increased Sarah's growing interest in design and building.

Throughout his adult life, William suffered from the symptoms of tuberculosis (known then as consumption). He was frail and had recurring bouts of breathing problems. He often would become ill in the winter and recover by spring. In 1880 William's father, Oliver, died. William was now the president of the Winchester Repeating Arms Company. The stress of serving as president took its toll on William and he became ill again in the winter of 1881. This time, however, William did not have a spring recovery. He died on March 7, 1881, at the age of 43, leaving Sarah a wealthy widow.

SARAH BUILDS HER MANSION

Losing her husband at a young age, following the loss of her only child Annie fifteen years earlier, was devastating to Sarah. The deep grief remained with her for the rest of her life. Although it has been reported that Sarah spent time in Europe after William's death, New Haven city directories from 1882 through 1884 list Sarah as living at 423 Prospect in New Haven.[2] Sarah's nephew, Winchester Bennett, said that his aunt stayed in New Haven for several years after her husband's death.[3]

Frank Carroll was Sarah's coachman in Connecticut. His wife Mary said that Mrs. Winchester's doctor had prescribed a change of climate in hopes of improving her health. The doctor also suggested that she engage in some absorbing activity or hobby, such

Workers at the Winchester estate. Courtesy, History San Jose.

as developing her former interest in architecture. [4]

Sarah took her doctor's advice and made the move to California in 1885. This would give her a fresh start and provide a climate that would be better for her ever-worsening rheumatoid arthritis. Later, Frank and Mary Carroll followed Sarah to California where Frank served as her coachman.

Sarah's sister, Nettie Sprague, had moved to California earlier in 1885, settling in Oakland, about 40 miles north of San Jose. Her husband, Homer Sprague, had been appointed the first president of Mills College for women there. Housing was provided for the Spragues on the Mills campus. Sarah and William had visited San Francisco some years before and liked the area, so when Nettie moved there, Sarah chose California as her new destination.

Her inheritance made Sarah a wealthy woman. In 1886 she purchased a small farmhouse with 45 acres of fruit and nut orchards in rural San Jose. The location in the Santa Clara valley reminded her of the Llanada Alavesa valley in the Pyrenees near the border of France and Spain, a place she and William had visited some years earlier. Sarah named her newly-purchased property Llanada Villa.

She immediately began to expand the house, planning for her other two sisters, Isabelle and Estelle, and their families to come out from Connecticut and live with her.

Roy Leib, son and partner of Sarah's attorney Samuel Franklin "Frank" Leib, said:

> *"She planned more and more rooms, at first, with some idea of providing separate family quarters in one connected structure for as many of her relatives as she could persuade to come west. The expected relatives didn't come, but the project afforded so much creative pleasure that she kept on with it."*[5]

As it turned out, her sisters did move to California but instead of moving in with Sarah, they decided they wanted to live in their own homes. San Jose was very isolated, so they chose to live further north, closer to the population centers. Sarah continued adding rooms to her house, providing living places for some of the household servants that she employed. She also took pleasure in running the fruit and nut farm, with the help of a foreman and field workers.

Once Sarah starting building, she rediscovered her love of architecture and woodworking. Returning to this love provided a distraction from her ever-present grief. William Winchester Merriman, Sarah's nephew, wrote that his aunt had decided to take on the hobby of architecture to get her mind off her past traumas.[6]

Sarah became her own architect, often sketching plans for innovative designs. Having no overall master plan, she sometimes found that, due to her lack of formal architectural training, her building ideas did not turn out as she envisioned. She would then have the workmen abandon the project and turn to another idea.

E. F. Wolters was a plumber at the Winchester House. He described her approach to planning and building the house:

> *"The house was merely Mrs. Winchester's hobby. She purchased and studied books on architecture and developed many innovative ideas in construction and design."*[7]

Sarah subscribed to one of the leading architectural journals of the time, *Architecture Record*, as shown in a canceled check.

Sarah's check for her subscription to the Architectural Record. Courtesy, History San Jose.

Carl Hansen was one of the sons of Sarah's foreman, John Hansen. Carl shared, "Sarah Winchester made a hobby of planning and building, and being a millionaire, she could afford to do it."[8]

From 1886 until the Great San Francisco Earthquake of 1906, Sarah expanded her house primarily because of her love of design. She enjoyed installing original features that enhanced the house. She also wanted to keep local carpenters and craftsmen employed and paid them much more than the standard wage.

Sarah's sister Isabelle lived with her husband and daughter about twenty miles north of San Jose in what today is the town of Los Altos. Isabelle's daughter Marion, known affectionately as Daisy, moved out of her parents' home in the late 1880s and went to live with her Aunt Sarah in San Jose. Daisy was about nineteen years old at the time. She and her aunt became very close, as Daisy served as Sarah's personal secretary for the next fifteen years. In 1903 Daisy married and moved away from San Jose.

Sarah's mansion before the 1906 earthquake. Courtesy, History San Jose.

In addition to her persistent grief, Sarah suffered from poor health primarily due to rheumatoid arthritis. She also had limited eyesight and decaying teeth. Her concern for her own health led her to purchase a copy of *Little Lessons in Corrective Eating* by Eugene Christian[9] from the Corrective Eating Society. The author suggests, "Human nutrition is the most important problem of life. The majority of diseases are traceable to wrong nutrition; while correct nutrition will render the body immune to most diseases." We do not know whether Sarah followed Christian's suggestions but she had an interest in healthy living.

Her health issues played a role in leading Sarah to choose a private life and not become part of local society. She was an anomaly in her community as she was an independent woman handling her own finances, an uncommon practice among women of her time. Also, it was virtually unknown for a woman to serve as her own architect and construction manager.

The Great Earthquake of 1906 in the San Francisco Bay Area heavily damaged the front section and upper floors of Sarah's home. Sarah was frustrated that the house suffered so much damage from the earthquake and blamed herself. She feared that her construction plans had not been adequate. Rather than repair the damaged rooms, she simply had unsafe parts of the house removed and boarded up other damaged areas.

The person most knowledgeable about the building of the mansion was Sarah's foreman, John Hansen. He gave the following explanation. "Mrs. Winchester talked of wrecking the place. She was persuaded instead to have the unsafe sections pulled off or boarded up."[10]

After the 1906 earthquake, a house Sarah also owned in nearby Atherton became her primary residence. The 1910 U. S. Census shows Sarah Winchester living in Township 3 in San Mateo County (today, the city of Atherton, 25 miles north of San Jose).[11]

Sarah often corresponded with her attorney, Frank Leib. These letters referred to Sarah visiting the house in San Jose while living in one of her other homes. One of Sarah's letters said, "I have been in San Jose very little for several months. The next time I am there for a few days, I shall try to see you."[12] Another stated, "I shall probably spend Thursday night in San Jose and

Sarah's mansion after the 1906 earthquake. Courtesy, History San Jose.

will look up the abstract which you request and send it to your office on Friday before I leave there again."[13]

After the 1906 earthquake Sarah abandoned her architectural hobby. For the remaining sixteen years of her life, the San Jose estate was run as a fruit and nut orchard by John Hansen.

Sarah now began to devote her time to creating a memorial for her husband that would help those in need. She decided that since tuberculosis was what took William's life, she would do all she could to help those suffering from the disease.

Fruit and nut orchards at Winchester. Courtesy, History San Jose.

CHAPTER 3

AN ARCHITECTURAL MARVEL

The eight-room farmhouse that Sarah Winchester purchased in 1886 was surrounded by 45 acres of orchards. As Sarah began her building, the modest farmhouse was gradually transformed into a classic example of American Queen Anne Revival architecture. The site afforded her sufficient room to add all of the features that characterized this style, which was popular in the United States from the 1880s to the 1910s.

Sarah added curved walls and tower rooms. Sections of the house were topped with turrets; cornices embellished the roof lines and windows. Balconies, porches and columns were added, each highly decorated. By the early 1900's the house had grown to a seven-story structure that fulfilled every aspect

Architectural details of Sarah's mansion. Courtesy, History San Jose.

of the American Queen Anne style. The mansion's crowning glory was a seven-story tower that reached 200 feet into the air. The tower and upper floors of the mansion did not survive the 1906 earthquake.

The interior of Sarah's mansion reflected the Aesthetic Movement that was prevalent in both Britain and the United States in the latter part of the nineteenth century. The movement, which embraced the concept of "art for art's sake," held that useful everyday objects could be beautiful. The idea was that beautiful surroundings were morally uplifting and improved people's quality of life. So Sarah incorporated into her house many decorated things such as doorknobs and hinges with intricate designs, and radiators that are pretty as well as useful. She took advantage of every opportunity to add decorative details.

Within her decorative designs, Sarah favored natural images: leaves, flowers, insects, birds. Sometimes the images are whimsical, sometimes reminiscent of other cultures: Persian, Moorish, Egyptian, Greek, Japanese. She ordered the finest quality fabrics, hardware and chandeliers, often importing materials from other countries.

The many fireplaces and mantelpieces in the house gave Sarah the opportunity to incorporate a variety of decorative forms. Some have intricate tiles interspersed with beveled crystal and carved wood. Some of the fireplaces used gas, others burned wood. Those that produced ashes had a small trap door at the bottom which could release all of the ash into a duct that led to the basement, where it could easily be cleaned out through another small door.

Guest reception hall. Courtesy, History San Jose.

Sarah's love of stained glass is apparent throughout the house. Her home contains about 100 stained-glass panels, and nearly 300 leaded clear-glass panels. The most intricate of the stained-glass windows have beveled crystal plus details called zipper cuts around the edges. Some windows are inlaid with small gems. Several rooms in the house contain spider-web windows, a design that was quite popular in Victorian homes.

In the grand ballroom are two art-glass windows with quotes from Shakespearean plays. One says "Wide unclasp the tables of their thoughts" and the other "These same thoughts people this little world." The first is from *Troilus and Cressida*, (Ulysses' description of Cressida's light-hearted mannerism); the second is from *Richard II* (spoken by Richard when he is in prison). The significance of these quotes to Sarah remains one of the mysteries of the Winchester Mansion. Sarah was well-versed in the works of Shakespeare. Her brother-in-law, Homer Sprague, was a Shakespearean scholar and professor who published a number of books on Shakespeare.

The grand ballroom, while not known for its size, has other interesting features. Sarah was an accomplished musician, and this room housed her organ. The intricate border on the wooden flooring in the ballroom is made with inlays of mahogany, ash, elm and oak. Other rooms in the house have similar parquet designs done in exotic woods.

Sarah chose Lincrusta wall coverings for many rooms in her mansion. This embossed wallpaper, made from a paste of gelled linseed oil and wood flour, was expensive and considered elegant for use in the finest buildings. It was installed in staterooms on the Titanic as well as in the White House in Washington, D.C. Sarah combined several patterns of Lincrusta

A hallway in the Winchester mansion. Courtesy, History San Jose.

in some rooms. She used it throughout the house, on ceilings as well as on walls.

The exact number of rooms in the mansion before the 1906 earthquake is not known, as there were no blueprints or floor plans from that time. Many staircases provide access to the maze of hallways, closets and alcoves and the variety of levels of the many rooms.

Sarah's limited mobility led to the construction of several staircases with steps rising just a few inches each, often necessitating the staircase to wind back and forth several times before reaching its destination. Her arthritis allowed her to lift her feet only two or three inches from the floor. The small steps made it possible for her to climb the stairs. Towards the end of Sarah's life, she was no longer able to walk and

Winding staircase with small steps. Courtesy, History San Jose.

used a wheelchair. She then had an electric elevator installed in the mansion, one of the first electric elevators ever placed in a private residence by the Otis Elevator Company. Previously she had added two hydraulic elevators to move plants and furnishings from floor to floor.

The small steps on the staircases were just one of Sarah's innovative moves to make life easier for herself and for those who worked for her. Because of Sarah's arthritic condition, it would have been difficult for her to use a bathtub. For the bathroom close to her bedroom she ordered a special shower which was called a "needle shower." The water came out of tiny holes in horseshoe-shaped pipes on two sides of the enclosure.

The laundry room was designed to lessen the work of the servants. Scrub boards were built into each of the three sinks, along with soap holders. Both hot and cold running water were available, a rarity in houses of that time.

Another aid for the servants was the brass corner plates set into each stair of the house. These prevented dust from collecting in the corners, which made cleaning much easier.

Sarah loved gardening and cared for her many indoor plants in two conservatory rooms. A unique flooring design in one of the conservatories made watering the plants easier. The wood panels of the floor were hinged and could be lifted to reveal an under-flooring of metal. Plants could be placed on the metal flooring to be watered. The water would then drain out via a pipe to join a complex drainage system that carried water away from the home's foundation.

Communication between Sarah and the staff in such a huge, sprawling house could be difficult. Sarah installed several systems to ease this problem. One was called an annunciator. Throughout the house she located a series of call buttons. When she pressed one of these buttons, a number would appear in a small window of the annunciator box, telling the staff where Sarah was in the house so they could answer her call.

Sarah's house also had a system of message tubes connecting the various levels. A person on one floor could be heard by someone on another floor simply by speaking into the tube.

By the beginning of the twentieth century, the Winchester estate had expanded to about 160 acres and was a self-sufficient operation with its own water supply and a variety of workshops. The property had a thirty-five foot water tower with a 10,000 gallon storage tank. Before electricity was installed, the house contained its own gas manufacturing plant. Carbide gas was produced by adding water to calcium carbide.

Sarah took as much care with the planning and planting of her gardens as she did with the interior of her mansion. She consulted several books on horticulture for ideas. Her formal gardens were Victorian in design, laid out with geometric exactness and using rows of neat hedges to define the areas. Sarah particularly loved both roses and daisies and used them extensively in her design. She also imported plants from around the world.

A team of gardeners led by Tommie Nishihara kept the gardens and grounds in good order. On the estate was a greenhouse where new plantings were nurtured. Sarah had several gazebos built on the grounds so that she could sit outside and enjoy her gardens.

Placed within the gardens are several fountains and a number of pieces of statuary. Best known is a statue of Chief Little Fawn, a Native American man holding his bow and arrow and looking toward a second statue, that of a deer. There are also statues of figures from Greek mythology, including one of the Greek goddess of agriculture, Demeter.

Much of the 160 acres of the Winchester estate was planted in orchards of plums, apricots and walnuts. A dehydrator powered by a coal furnace was used to process the plums and apricots. The dried fruit was sold by distributors at markets in San Jose.

CHAPTER 4

SARAH BUILDS HER HOSPITAL

When Sarah received her inheritance following William's death, the decision was made that her finances would be managed by two of her relatives who handled finances for the Winchester Repeating Arms Company. One was Thomas Bennett, William's sister's husband; the other was William Converse, the husband of Sarah's sister Mary. After moving to California, Sarah decided to manage her own money and from that time forward she took control of her financial affairs.

Sarah's wealth came not only from her inheritance, but also from her wise investments in real estate, stocks, and bonds. Her many real estate investments included houses for her relatives, her employees, and herself, as well as properties purchased for investment purposes. She also owned a houseboat that she kept moored in San Francisco Bay. She lived on the boat for a short time following the 1906 earthquake.

Sarah's attorney in California, Frank Leib, served as her agent and advisor for her financial transactions. Hundreds of letters between Sarah and Leib demonstrate Sarah's active involvement in her financial affairs.

At the time of Sarah's death in 1922, her estate was valued at $2,914,159, as filed with the court of the County of Santa Clara (about $44 million in 2019 dollars).[14] The assets making up her estate attest to the sophistication of her investments. She owned six separate residences, all of substantial size. She owned stocks and bonds from 55 separate institutions, not including the Winchester Repeating Arms Company. Her 20,820 shares of Winchester stock were valued at $1,244,650 at the time of her death.

Two of attorney Frank Leib's major clients were Sarah Winchester and Jane Stanford. Jane Stanford was the widow of Leland Stanford, railroad tycoon and former governor of California. The Stanfords' only child, Leland Jr., died at the age of 15 from typhoid. The Stanfords founded Stanford University as a memorial to their son. Perhaps this contributed to Sarah's desire to create a lasting memorial for her husband.

After the 1906 earthquake, Sarah began to devote most of her energy to planning for such a memorial.

Since William had died from tuberculosis, Sarah wanted to help those who suffered from the disease, and decided to make that the focus for a memorial to honor William.

Tuberculosis (also known as TB) is a disease in which bacteria invades the lungs, sometimes making it difficult for a person to breathe. Throughout history the disease was known by other names including the white plague (because victims became very pale) and consumption (because the disease devoured or consumed the person, causing a gradual wasting away of the victim's body). Scientists believe the disease has been in existence for over 2,500 years. By the 1800s, tuberculosis was the leading cause of death in the United States. TB germs are put into the air when a person with TB coughs, sneezes or speaks. Poor hygiene in urban areas, where people lived in close proximity, advanced the spread of the disease.

Throughout most of history, the root cause of TB was not known. In 1882 Prussian physician Robert Koch discovered that the disease was caused by bacteria and was spread by contact with infected people. This discovery led to the need for isolating those with the disease, which in turn led to the creation of sanatoriums. Sanatoriums allowed TB sufferers to receive specialized care and sunshine. It was believed that fresh air helped effect a cure. The first sanatorium in the United States was the Adirondack Cottage Sanatorium (also known as the Trudeau Sanatorium) at Saranac Lake, New York, founded by Dr. Edward Trudeau.

In addition to sanatoriums, doctors in large urban areas realized the need for specialized hospitals to isolate tuberculosis patients. This concept became prevalent in the beginning of the twentieth century. This was the time period when Sarah helped fill this need by funding a tuberculosis hospital. Since New Haven, Connecticut, was the ancestral home for both the Winchesters and the Pardees, Sarah decided that the memorial would be appropriately located there.

The General Hospital Society of Connecticut was founded in 1826 to provide medical care for residents of the New Haven region. Members of the Winchester family were benefactors of the Hospital Society. In their annual report for 1908, the Hospital Society stated, "We again call attention to what seems to us to be the greatest present need of the community, a ward for the care of advanced cases of uncomplicated pulmonary tuberculosis."[15]

The need for a tuberculosis facility is emphasized in the "Admission of Patients" directive in the Annual Report, where it states, "Persons suffering from uncomplicated pulmonary tuberculosis are not admitted to the wards."[16]

Sarah most likely read either the annual report or possibly an article describing the need for a hospital in the *New Haven Register,* a newspaper to which she subscribed from her home in California. It is believed that this was the impetus for her choice of a tuberculosis hospital as a memorial for her husband.

Eli Whitney (the grandson of the inventor of the cotton gin) was the president of the General Hospital Society of Connecticut in 1909. Sarah began her quest by writing a letter to Mr. Whitney on November 6, 1909.[17] In the letter she states her dominant purpose is to find some worthy and enduring memorial for her husband. She decided an institution for the treatment of tuberculosis is "in every way the best thing I could do." She said she would like to give the General Hospital Society of Connecticut $300,000 to carry out her purpose. As soon as she received and approved a general plan (not necessarily a detailed one), she would send the check. Sarah's $300,000 initial donation would be worth about $8.3 million in 2019 dollars.

Apparently a general plan was almost immediately sent to Sarah, for on December 1, 1909, she mailed a check for $300,000 to the General Hospital Society. On December 7 Eli Whitney wrote a letter to Sarah in which he acknowledged receipt of the check.[18]

As with most of her charitable donations, Sarah wished that her donation to the General Hospital Society be kept confidential. Although her identity was exposed before the hospital opened in 1918, many documents refer to Sarah as "the donor."

Sarah's attorney and counselor Frank Leib was also involved in the correspondence with the Hospital Society. On December 23, 1909, President Whitney sent a letter to Leib:

> *"This is one of the most liberal gifts that the hospital has ever received, and it has been appropriated to the most useful purpose possible at this present time. There is at present no such ward or institution in the State for the treatment of advanced cases of tuberculosis as is provided for by this gift."*[19]

In 1910 Sarah donated an additional $300,000 to the General Hospital Society of Connecticut to be added to her original donation. Construction on the new hospital began in 1911. The site for the hospital was chosen in the Allingtown district of West Haven (a suburb of New Haven), Connecticut. On advice from the staff of the Trudeau Sanatorium, the architect firm of Scopes & Feustmann was hired to design the new hospital.

In 1913, Yale University formed an alliance with the General Hospital Society of Connecticut. Responsibility for the hospital shifted from Eli Whitney, president of the General Hospital Society, to Dr. George Blumer, dean of the Yale Medical School.

Part of Sarah's wish for the memorial hospital was that it would serve patients of all economic levels.

Sarah's personal physician, Charles Wayland, often spoke for her:

> *"It is her [Sarah's] wish to have the ward beds at such a reasonable rate that the poor may have access to the wards. It is her [Sarah's] desire that no hardship should come to the poorer class of patients because of their inability to meet the financial part of their obligation."*[20]

As the building progressed, it was determined that additional funds would be needed. Sarah responded to the need. By the time the tuberculosis hospital opened in 1918, her total donations amounted to $1,325,000 (about $33 million in 2019 dollars).[21] All of Sarah's donations were aggregated into the tuberculosis fund of the General Hospital Society of Connecticut. Monies from this fund paid for the construction of the hospital and for ongoing operating costs.

Construction was completed in 1918. The William Wirt Winchester Tuberculosis Annex of the New Haven Hospital was a three-story structure designed to serve 126 patients. It consisted of four buildings made of brick and steel. The *New Haven Register* describes the hospital as "the best, most up-to-date and most improved institution of its kind in the country."[22]

Dedication ceremonies for the hospital were held on April 4, 1918. Unfortunately, Sarah's health did not allow her to attend. Sarah had previously expressed her wishes for the dedication ceremony in a letter from Charles Wayland to George Blumer:

> *"It is the expressed wish of the donor that the dedication exercises be performed in a simple and unostentatious manner; that no lengthy eulogy of a personal character be spoken, carrying the idea of simplicity in every sense of the word."*[23]

The letter also showed Sarah's great care for the less fortunate. Dr. Wayland said, "the donor expresses a great delight that those who are poor sufferers from the dreaded tuberculosis may receive proper care and scientific treatment, as this has been the one great aim of a long life."[24]

A memorial plaque was unveiled at the ceremony. Several weeks after the ceremony, George Blumer

Courtesy, History San Jose

wrote to Sarah, "Even though you were not able to be present, you can, I am sure, rest assured that you have been responsible for an institution which will be of the greatest possible benefit and service to the people of New Haven for many years to come."[25]

In 1917 the United States entered World War I. By the beginning of 1918, the War Department desperately needed a hospital to treat soldiers returning from Europe with tuberculosis. They requested to lease the brand-new William Wirt Winchester Tuberculosis Annex. The Board of the General Hospital Society of Connecticut felt it was their duty to accommodate this request, but first needed to obtain permission from Sarah Winchester.

On February 1, 1918, George Blumer received the following telegram from Charles Wayland: "The donor consents to the hospital being used by the Government as expressed in your telegram yesterday."[26]

The hospital opened on May 18, 1918, with a new temporary name of United States Army General Hospital No. 16. Lieutenant-Colonel Alexius M. Forster was the commanding officer. In the next few months, the number of hospital beds was increased to provide space for 650 patients. This hospital was designated as the primary Army treatment center for tuberculosis.[27] Doctors sent to other Army tuberculosis hospitals were trained here.

Little did Sarah know that her memorial gift would provide such a major benefit to the U.S. Army. In fact, it would be nine more years before the hospital was returned to the General Hospital Society of Connecticut in 1927. It would be five years after Sarah's death in 1922 before the name was changed from United States Army General Hospital No. 16 to its originally intended name of the William Wirt Winchester Tuberculosis Annex of the New Haven Hospital.

For the next twenty years, the hospital served the civilian population of the New Haven area. Sarah's generosity insured that no one was turned away because of lack of funds. Thousands of patients received treatment. A hospital brochure confirms Sara's intentions:

> *"Mrs. Sarah L. Winchester realized the importance of hospital facilities for the treatment of persons who have tuberculosis. [It is] a private institution, privately endowed, and designed especially for patients of moderate means."*[28]

The hospital also operated a summer camp known as Camp Happyland. The camp was designed "to take care of children coming from families where there is tuberculosis and whose physical condition is such that rest, fresh air and good food are essential."[29]

Sarah's Hospital. Courtesy, The Archives of Yale New Haven Hospital.

Nurses' Quarters. Courtesy, U.S. Department of Health & Human Services, National Library of Medicine.

A typical day at Camp Happyland shows a busy schedule.[30]

9:15	Inspection by camp director
9:30	Group singing
10:00	Crackers and milk
10:15	Sunbaths
10.45	Girls swimming
11:15	Boys swimming
11:45	Wash for dinner
12:00	Dinner
1:00	Rest hour
2:00	Bananas and milk
3:00	Activities: dramatics, handicraft, nature study, toy making, short hikes, girl scouts
4:20	Ready for supper
4:50	Colors
5:00	Supper
5:45	Clinic
6:30	Camp fire
7:00	Taps. Showers and to bed
7:30	Lights out

The camp was funded by the William Wirt Winchester Fund established through Sarah's donations, and was free to the children. Due to the consistent nourishment and focus on healthy living, many of the children who arrived in a weakened condition left the camp with beneficial weight gains.

The tuberculosis rate began declining in the 1920s due to increased public health campaigns. In 1944 Albert Schatz, Elizabeth Bugie, and Selman Waksman discovered that streptomycin was an antibiotic that was effective in treating tuberculosis. This discovery led to a sharp decline in cases of tuberculosis. According to the U.S. Centers for Disease Control, the death rate from tuberculosis in 1915 was 140.1 persons per 100,000 population. By 1945 the death rate had decreased to 39.9 persons per 100,000 population.[31]

Due to the decrease in cases of tuberculosis, it was determined that the operation of the William Wirt Winchester Tuberculosis Annex of the New Haven Hospital was no longer economically feasible. The hospital was sold to the U.S. Veterans Administration in 1948 and the William Wirt Winchester Fund was then reassigned. The Grace New Haven Hospital Annual Report announced the changes.[32] (In 1945 the New Haven Hospital merged with the Grace Hospital).

The third floor in the Tompkins Pavilion was designated as the William Wirt Winchester Annex – Surgical Division. The third floor of the Isolation Building was designated as the William Wirt Winchester Annex— Medical Division. Patients with tuberculosis and allied chest conditions were cared for on these two floors and income from the Winchester fund would be used to defray the expenses of these patients.

By 1956 all the components that were supported by the Winchester Fund were consolidated into the Winchester Chest Clinic. The clinic's mission was to "provide diagnostic, supervisory and treatment service for patients with tuberculosis in the Greater New Haven area at no cost to any of them coming to the Clinic."[33]

Today the clinic treats patients with chest and lung ailments as well as those with tuberculosis. Sarah would be greatly pleased that the Winchester Chest Clinic is still serving humanity in 2019, nearly 100 years after Sarah's death, and that William's name lives on.

CHAPTER 5

THE MANSION AFTER SARAH'S DEATH

Many years of rheumatoid arthritis had taken a toll on Sarah's body, and by the summer of 1922 she was confined to her bed. The end of Sarah's life came on the fifth of September. At her side was her long-time personal secretary and companion Henrietta Sivera. The official cause of death was listed as "chronic myocarditis."[34]

Stories had begun to circulate about Sarah and her large house many years before her death. An article in the 1895 *San Jose Evening News* was the first time the story appeared in print.

> "...Ten years ago the handsome residence was apparently ready for occupancy, but improvements and additions are

Henrietta Sivera with Sarah's foreman, John Hansen. Courtesy, History San Jose.

constantly being made, for the reason, it is said, that the owner of the house believes that when it is entirely completed, she will die."[35]

The story was repeated in 1896 in *American Architect and Building News*.[36] This was the era of yellow journalism when newspapers were more interested in sensational stories than in well-researched facts. During Sarah's lifetime, other articles were published with the story morphing into her being told by a medium that she had been cursed by the spirits of all those killed with Winchester rifles and the only way to protect herself was to continue building nonstop.

Two days after Sarah's death, her obituary appeared in the *San Jose Mercury*:[37]

> *"Mrs. Sarah Winchester, for nearly 40 years a resident of this locality, passed away yesterday at her home on the Los Gatos road. Mrs. Winchester was the widow of William Wirth [sic] Winchester, son of the founder of the Winchester Arms Company of Connecticut, who succeeded the latter as the head of that institution.*
>
> *After the death of her husband, Mrs. Winchester devoted her time to works of charity and was largely responsible for the maintenance of several charitable*

institutions and hospitals. Among those benefactions, one in which she was particularly interested was the tuberculosis section of the Connecticut State Hospital.

A woman of the most retiring nature, extremely sensitive and opposed to publicity of any character, Mrs. Winchester never permitted any notice of her charitable activities to be made public. By her death, however, many of the unfortunate people in all parts of the country will have lost a faithful friend and benefactor."

Sarah's obituary made no mention of her building her house continuously to please the spirits of those killed by the Winchester rifle. In fact, it made no mention of any of the stories that had appeared in previous years. There was little mention of the house or Sarah in local papers during the next eight months.

In Sarah's will she left to her niece, Marion Marriott, "all of my pictures, furniture, household goods, jewelry and paraphernalia." However, Sarah did not designate a beneficiary for her San Jose home and its 161 surrounding acres of orchards.[38] It was to be sold as part of the estate by her trustee, the Union Trust Company of San Francisco.

On December 16, 1922, the house and surrounding land were sold to real estate developer T. C. Barnett for $135,531. Barnett subdivided the estate into two parcels; the parcel without the house sold quickly. During the next five months, only one buyer showed interest in the parcel with the house. That was John Brown, an innovative amusement-park entrepreneur. In early May 1923 he signed a ten-year lease with an option to purchase the property.

John Brown of J. H. Brown & Co. had invented and patented the Backety-Back Scenic Railway in 1904.[39] It was a roller coaster that had a series of two dead-end inclines that caused the trains to stop, reverse direction, and then roll to a track on a lower level without any mechanical switching mechanisms. It premiered at the Jamestown Exposition in Virginia in 1907 and then was moved to the Crystal Beach Park near Niagara Falls, Ontario, Canada.

The Backety-Back was a pioneering roller coaster which became known as a "shuttle roller coaster." Today, many of the best-known roller coasters in the world are based on Brown's innovative design.

Brown originally planned to turn the mansion into a full-scale amusement park with a roller coaster inside the house. An article in the *Palo Alto Times* stated:

> *"Plans for the construction of a $200,000 amusement park on the Winchester estate, near San Jose, were announced here today.*

The park will be built by J. H. Brown & Co., an Eastern amusement concern. The old home, containing 142 rooms, will be the central concession. A swimming pool, scenic railway, and a children's playground will be some of the features of the park."[40]

However, for reasons unknown, the plans for the full-scale amusement park never materialized. Instead the house was opened in 1923 as a stand-alone tourist attraction which became known as the Winchester Mystery House.

Brown decided that the best way to promote the new attraction was to advertise it as a haunted house. The beginning of the 20th century had seen the start of family amusement parks. An inexpensive way to attract families to these parks without spending a lot on elaborate mechanical equipment was to advertise a haunted house. There was a "spook house" in Crystal Beach Park, home of Brown's Backety-Back Scenic Railway. This may have sparked Brown's idea of focusing on the oddities of the Winchester mansion as a "mystery house."

The rumors of spirits and hauntings had started during Sarah's lifetime. The new attraction featured these rumors as well as the unusual construction features that were a result of the 1906 earthquake and Sarah's unique designs. Signs of the occult and occurrences of the number 13 were added in order to enhance its connection to the paranormal, believing that this would attract more customers.

At that time, portraying stories as fact in the promotion of a tourist attraction was a common practice. Additionally, in the 1920s the historic building preservation movement had not yet been started. The National Historic Preservation Act, which established the National Register of Historic Places, was not enacted by Congress until 1966. The California State Historical Landmark Program did not begin until 1931.

It is likely that the Winchester mansion would have been demolished in the 1920s if John Brown had not found a way to make it into a paying proposition. Only through his determined efforts at that time was the house spared for future generations.

Ruth Amet of the *San Jose Mercury* was invited to visit the house before it opened. She was given a tour and told all of the promotional stories that had been devised. She wrote a lengthy article that was featured in the *San Jose Mercury* on May 27, 1923, reporting the stories she had been told.[41]

The grand opening occurred on June 30, 1923. From that day on the stories about Sarah and her house have been told and retold to the point that they are often treated as fact.

CHAPTER 6

MISCONCEPTIONS ABOUT THE MANSION

The stories about the Winchester Mystery House and Sarah have become a part of San Jose history. The house is the best known landmark in the area. These stories have attracted and continue to attract tourists to San Jose. The website of the San Jose Visitors and Convention Bureau lists the Winchester Mystery House as the number one "must-see" attraction in San Jose.[42]

When Sarah settled in San Jose she was friendly with her neighbors and business associates. According to Scott Bailey, a tour supervisor at the Winchester Mystery House in the 1970s, Sarah was a friend of the Bishop family and Albert Schurra.[43] The Bishops were connected to the C&H Sugar Company. Albert Schurra founded a candy shop in San Jose which closed in 2018 after 106 years in business.

Ralph Rambo was the nephew of a west coast employee for the Winchester Repeating Arms Company. He said "Mrs. Winchester was neither cold nor distant in her early years of valley residence. She was a highly sensitive lady and the cruel rumors even then in circulation disturbed and hurt her. Eventually all this idle gossip reached her ears and as it persisted she withdrew closer into her multi-storied shell."[44]

As rumors about Sarah circulated, she chose to keep to herself more often and to avoid social engagements. One factor that led to the circulation of rumors was her connection to the Winchester rifle.

Mary Jo Ignoffo, author of *Captive of the Labyrinth,* concluded that one of the reasons Sarah moved to California was to obtain a higher level of anonymity than she had in New Haven. However, Sarah underestimated the fame of the Winchester name and the interest that her neighbors would take in her residency in San Jose. Additionally, Ignoffo believes that newspapers linked deaths from the Winchester rifle to Sarah. The fact that Winchester rifles had been used in the subjugation of the Native American nations made Sarah Winchester, in the eyes of some people, guilty of atrocities.[45]

As her arthritic condition worsened, her arms and legs became gnarled. This, plus her dental problems, added to her desire to avoid public appearances.

Sarah's desire for seclusion, in addition to the fact that

she was a single woman building a large and unique house on her own, led to more gossip and speculation in her community. This in turn led to stories in the media which over time were treated as facts.

Although it is hard to pinpoint the exact moment the stories started, curious neighbors and journalists devised explanations of the construction that they observed. They saw large additions being made to the house behind the tall fences that surrounded the grounds. The appearance of towers and cupolas added to the speculation.

Newspaper and magazine articles appeared in publications not only in California but throughout the country. Few of the articles about Sarah and her house quoted people who knew her. Those few articles that did quote people who knew her paint a different picture than the multitude of anonymous reports. The quotes from those closest to Sarah offer alternative explanations to the stories that were reported in the media. Likewise, letters in archives from people who directly knew Sarah do the same.

Part of the story about the house was that construction was continuous. The *Dayton* (Ohio) *Daily News* reported "The sound of hammers never ceased as up to 16 carpenters at a time worked 24 hours every day, including Sundays and holidays, for 38 years."[46] Sarah did hire workmen to accomplish specific building tasks. However, the majority of the building took place between 1886 and 1906, and was accomplished during regular daytime working hours.

Carl Hansen, the son of foreman John Hansen, wrote, "There were periods up to about six years when she did no building at all. I am sure that she was not worried about anything happening to her if she stopped building."[47]

Plumber E. F. Wolters related that Mrs. Winchester was annoyed at a newspaper story published in 1901 about her connection to the spirits, and afterwards she dismissed all the builders. Operations did not resume until the following year.[48]

Attorney Roy Leib stated that Sarah did not hire a single carpenter after her house was damaged in the earthquake of 1906. Workers to clean up the debris and maintain the house were hired, but no artisan carpenters were employed on new projects.[49]

Some of the curious features of the house were attributed to her desire to confuse the evil spirits or to follow the directions given her by the good spirits. For example, the *Los Angeles Times* reported "In her battle against evil spirits, she constructed some stairways that lead to dead-ends, and doors that open to blank walls. One 'door to nowhere' connects the second story of the house to the front yard, but there are no stairs outside."[50]

There are practical explanations for the oddities in the house. Architectural irregularities came about in response to damage by the 1906 earthquake, her lack of formal training in architecture, and adaptations to her physical disabilities. Foreman John Hansen said:

> *"This [damage from the 1906 earthquake] would account for the outside door on the third floor, which couldn't possibly be of use to anyone but a parachutist. There also are plausible explanations for some of the other paradoxes. The bar protected inside windows were undoubtedly on the outside of the house until further building enclosed them. The exterior second-story water faucets probably had window boxes under them. The room full of 'trapdoors' was an upper-floor conservatory with an ingenious double floor for drainage purposes."*[51]

Attorney Roy Leib confirmed that some of the oddities of the house were due to Sarah's lack of formal architectural training. At that time in history, very few women had received formal training. "When she made mistakes, as she was bound to do with her amateur knowledge and erratic methods of construction, she blithely demolished them and started over, hid them with drapes, built right over them, or simply left them undisguised."[52]

Neighbor Minnie Hall believed, "The so-called secret passageways – supposedly for ghosts – were none other than shortcuts between rooms for the use of the servants."[53]

Ralph Rambo gave the reason for the two-inch high steps in the house. "In her 70's and 80's, Mrs. Winchester was a victim of advanced arthritis and neuritis and these low steps matched her reduced abilities."[54]

In order to support the marketing strategy developed in 1923, it is believed that changes were made to the house. Two of Sarah's relatives thought this was the case. Sarah's nephew William Merriman said, "Many of the bizarre things in the house had been added after her death to make the house intriguing when it opened up for public tours."[55]

Donald Robesky, Sarah's great-nephew by marriage, said, "I understand certain additions were made to the house after Mrs. Winchester's death."[56]

James Perkins, a carpenter at the Winchester House, confirmed this as well by stating, "Some of the more irregular features which have made the house a world-famed oddity were built after Mrs. Winchester's death."[57]

Some people thought that Sarah was a spiritualist. The *Sikeston* (Missouri) *Standard* said "…Mrs. Winchester was a devout spiritualist and the house was built as the Spirits instructed her to build it."[58] They also believed that she had never attended a church.

Both of the women who served as Sarah's personal secretary denied this. Marion Marriott, Sarah's niece and first personal secretary, told her son-in-law, Donald Robesky, that Sarah Winchester was never a spiritualist.[59] Sarah's second personal secretary, Henrietta Sivera, always firmly denied that Sarah had any spiritualist leanings.[60]

Sarah was an Episcopalian. She had allowed Reverend Redmond Payne to start a congregation in a vacant room in a house that she owned near the town of Los Altos. Eventually the congregation was able to have their own building, and the Reverend invited Sarah to attend the first service there:

> *"My dear Mrs. Winchester, I am enclosing the announcement of the completion of our little Episcopal church in Los Altos. We are very proud of it architecturally and every other way. I thought you might feel a particular interest in this, our first service. I hope you will find it possible to come for we shall all be very glad to see you there."*[61]

A noted feature of the Winchester House is the room at the center of the house known as the "blue room" or the "séance room." The *Dearborn* (Michigan) *Independent* described the room as "entered by a plain door...Two small windows to inclosed skylights are steel barred. Noteworthy here is a capacious closet in which were kept numerous wondrously colored silk and satin gowns each having, by virtue of it's [sic] hue, a specific relationship to a spirit guide."[62]

It is said that no one other than Sarah was allowed into the room. However, descriptions of séances, which were not uncommon at that time, say that they were held as a group experience led by a medium.

Two of Sarah's acquaintances report that the room had other uses. Sarah's foreman, John Hansen, said:

> "The blue séance room, instead of being sacred to the person of its mistress, was actually used by almost everyone except Mrs. Winchester. It served as [my] bedroom for eight months, then in turn was used by the caretaker, a Japanese cook and his wife, one of the nurses, and the chauffeur."[63]

Ralph Rambo confirmed this to be the case.[64]

The number 13 is often associated with the occult. According to an article in *California Camper*, "The number 13, which Sarah felt was especially lucky for her and the good spirits, was used constantly: 13 panes in a window, 13 windows in a room, 13 holders in a candelabra [sic], 13 panels in a wall, 13 coathooks in a closet, 13 steps in a staircase. The list is endless."[65]

Sarah's neighbor, Minnie Hall, believed that the number 13 held no special symbolism for Sarah.[66]

James Perkins, a carpenter at the Winchester House, believed, "The number '13' in chandeliers, the numbers of bathrooms, windows, ceiling panels and other things were certainly put in after Mrs. Winchester died."[67]

A bell tower with a single bell is located in the center of the mansion. It was reported that the bell was rung every night at midnight to summon the spirits, and again at 2 a.m. to release them for departure. Of all the wild stories printed in newspapers, the story published in the *American Weekly* may be the wildest.

> *"The Japanese bell ringer carried an expert watch...Every day he phoned to an astronomical observatory and checked the correctness of his chronometers, from which in turn, he set his watch. The countryside could not understand why the Winchester bell always rang at the hour of midnight... That is all that a properly behaved ghost needs to know about time."*[68]

Other practical reasons for the bell tower are noted. Neighbor Minnie Hall recollected, "The only time I ever heard the bell ringing was for calling workers in from the gardens and orchards for meals, never at other times."[69]

Ralph Rambo indicated, "The bell in the belfry was a most practical signal, not for 'nightly ghostly assembly' but for a fire alarm and as a start and stop signal for the workers in her distant prune and apricot orchards."[70]

It has often been reported that when William died Sarah inherited $20 million and would receive dividends of $1,000 a day. According to *People Magazine* "William died in 1881, making Sarah a widow at 41 and an heiress to $20 million (more than $490 million today)."[71]

When Sarah passed away in 1922, her estate was valued at just under three million dollars. Because of the common misconception about the size of her original inheritance, she was accused of foolishly spending most of her money on her house.

According to the Connecticut Probate Court, William Winchester's estate was worth $362,329 at the time of his death.[72] This amount includes $300,000 of Winchester Repeating Arms stock that belonged to William's mother Jane and would go to Sarah upon Jane's death. This was still a great deal of money, translating to about $9 million in 2019 dollars.

In addition to the money Sarah inherited, she also received income from stock dividends in the Winchester Repeating Arms Company. An article in *Coronet Magazine* stated: "She [Sarah] . . . had an income of $1,000 a day."[73]

In 1952 Harold Williamson researched the history of the Winchester Repeating Arms Company and produced *Winchester, The Gun that Won the West*. Appendix G-4 shows the balance sheet as of December 31, 1880, for the Repeating Arms Company with a

Probate record of William Winchester
source: LDS microfilm #1405965.

total net worth of only $3,044,102.

Appendix F of Williamson's book shows an annual dividend table. Between 1881 and 1897, Sarah received average daily dividends of $68 (about $1,860 in 2019 dollars). In 1898 Sarah's mother-in-law died leaving Sarah 2,200 more shares of the company stock. Between 1898 and 1914, Sarah received average daily dividends of $554 (about $15,500 in 2019 dollars). Not only did her number of shares increase after Jane

Winchester's death, but the profits of the Winchester Repeating Arms Company grew significantly during this period.

The stories about the Winchester House and the spirits led some to believe that Sarah was crazy. Who but a crazed person would believe that the spirits were giving her directions and that she would live on as long as she kept building? Sarah's acquaintances did not believe this was so.

Attorney Roy Leib said, "Mrs. Winchester was as sane and clear-headed a woman as I have ever known."[74]

Carl and Ted Hansen were the two sons of Sarah's foreman John Hansen and grew up in a house next to the Winchester mansion. They both felt efforts to dispute all of the stories told about Sarah Winchester were in vain.

Carl believed:

> *"So much fiction has been written about Mrs. Winchester that I am afraid most people are not interested in the facts. I talked with Mrs. Winchester. She seemed entirely normal to me. It would take hours to contradict all the wild tales that have been told about Mrs. Winchester, so I will close by saying that they are not true or have very simple explanations."*[75]

And brother Ted agreed:

> *"For several years it has been my personal policy not to grant any interviews or to hold any discussions concerning Mrs. Winchester. It is nearly fifty years since Mrs. Winchester's death and the many stories (many which were published long before her death) have become so popular that any attempt to refute these stories is more or less futile."*[76]

*Ted and Carl Hansen along with Sarah's great-niece Margaret.
Courtesy, History San Jose.*

CHAPTER 7

THE KIND AND GENEROUS SARAH

Although Sarah chose not to mingle with the community, she was generous and kind to all of the people in her life. All references uncovered reveal this to be the case.

Minnie Hall and her family were Sarah Winchester's closest neighbors when Minnie was a child. Minnie spent many afternoons at the Winchester property, playing with Carl and Ted Hansen, the sons of Mrs. Winchester's foreman John Hansen. Sarah was very fond of Minnie; perhaps Minnie reminded her of the daughter that she had lost. Later in her life, Minnie reflected on Sarah:

> *"Mrs. Winchester never entertained me in the house but often we sat in her beautiful*

> *gardens, watching the horses and buggies go by, we had such enjoyable visits. I was always 'Little Minnie' to Mrs. Winchester. She was the dearest old lady to ever come along in my lifetime. Everybody loved her dearly and were loyal to her as anyone could be. There was so much harmony on the place amongst all the help."*[77]

Minnie beautifully described Sarah's humble way of helping:

> *"In an era when neighbors helped neighbors in time of need or tragedy, an anonymous donation appeared. When community church women held a rummage sale, Mrs. Winchester often donated boxes of clothing she had bought in town."*[78]

Elmer Jensen was Sarah's newspaper delivery boy, bringing the *San Jose Evening News* to her home. He recalled one conversation that conveyed Sarah's compassion:

> *"I recall one occasion when I called on her at her home as a small boy and requested permission to shoot robins with my air gun. Of course she refused me, but I will always remember her giving me the complete story of the life of the robins and how they were hunger-driven from the snow and ice-cold slopes of the Sierras*

down to the warm valleys. It made such an impression on me that never again did I shoot at a songbird."[79]

Sarah not only loved robins but was appreciative of the natural environment, including the unique forests of redwood trees in California. Andrew P. Hill was a well-known Northern California photographer, painter, and conservationist. Concerned about the protection of the redwoods, in 1899 Hill founded the Sempervirens Club. The club's goal was to raise funds for the purchase of land to create a state park in the Santa Cruz Mountains (today known as Big Basin Redwoods State Park). Sarah supported Hill's efforts and donated $500 to the Sempervirens Club.[80]

Frank Leib was Sarah's long-time lawyer and financial counselor who eventually became her friend. Roy Leib was Frank's son. For many years he practiced law with his father. When Frank retired, Roy took over the family business. Both Leibs spoke about Sarah's kindness.

Frank said about Sarah:

"Mrs. Winchester was all that a woman should be, and nothing that a good woman should not be. She would have disliked any notice of her good deeds, although there were many. If there is a heaven, there she would surely be."[81]

Roy noticed her generosity:

> *"She contributed to many charities regularly and others on the spur of the moment, anonymously whenever possible. She habitually sent loads of fruits and nuts from her trees to an orphanage. When her coachman died she gave his family money to buy a home."*[82]

Ralph Rambo was the nephew of Ned Rambo, the first San Francisco agent for the Winchester Repeating Arms Company. When Sarah first moved to California, Ned spent time acquainting her with the countryside. Ralph, an accomplished author himself, grew up hearing many stories about Sarah from his uncle.

> *"The full scope of her generosity, charity and many kindly acts will forever remain unknown and such was her sincere desire. [She made] unheralded trips to old Cupertino church where my mother and other women of the Ladies Aid Society collected used clothing for the local poors' [sic] children."*[83]

James Perkins, a carpenter who worked on Sarah's house, thought very highly of his employer:

> *"I want the whole world to know that Mrs. Winchester was a very well educated woman – one who loved music and played*

*Samuel "Frank" Leib, Sarah's attorney and friend.
Courtesy, History San Jose.*

brilliantly herself. She was generous and kind and treated all her help as if they were members of the family."[84]

Sarah's head gardener was Tommie Nishahara. At a time in California history when there was much prejudice against Japanese-Americans, Sarah was one of the few wealthy residents who was open to hiring workers of all ethnic backgrounds. Tommie was so appreciative of his relationship with Sarah that his granddaughter, Ida, was given the middle name of Winchester. Neighbor Minnie Hall recollected that Tommie was particularly saddened when Sarah died.[85]

Tommie's granddaughter, Ida Winchester Nishihara. Courtesy, History San Jose.

CHAPTER 8

LETTERS TO JENNIE

Although much of Sarah's business correspondence has been preserved, there are very few personal letters written by her still in existence. The Connecticut Historical Society has preserved in their collection two letters written in 1898 by Sarah to her sister-in-law Jennie Bennett (William's sister) who was still living in New Haven, Connecticut.[86]

These letters are interesting because of the mundane nature of the topics discussed by Sarah. They are a good representation of how ordinary Sarah was, with no signs of eccentricity or obsessions.

Sarah tells Jennie that she has decided to give up drinking coffee and has been tired and listless. "I don't know what to attribute this very somnolent condition, unless it is the result of having left off drinking coffee. In some respects I think I am better for the abstinence but it is horrible to be so dull and good for nothing."

The house that Sarah shared with William in Connecticut was known by the family as "the house on the hill." This is the house where baby Annie was born and died at six weeks of age. She writes to Jennie, "I often wonder whether the house on the hill is closed or whether anyone is occupying it. There is so much of sadness inseparable from thoughts of all these things that I try not to allow myself to dwell on them long."

At the time these letters were written, Jennie and William's mother had recently passed away. Sarah had given her mother-in-law a number of silver pieces. She requested that Jennie have some of the pieces inscribed showing that they were gifts from Sarah to her mother-in-law Jane. She wrote, "Nothing would please me better than to know that thus inscribed they would be heirlooms for your children."

Sarah, like any homeowner, was concerned with the plaster on her walls. "I have such dreadful luck with plaster. I had had so much trouble with ordinary plaster, that I thought I would try adamant [a new type of plaster] and had two rooms done with it. It seemed all right for a time but now in the room I had used for a guest room, it has loosened so as to be unsafe that I shall have it all removed from the walls and replastered."

Sarah also was not satisfied with the plumbing in her house. "I have been looking closely into the matter of sanitary plumbing and find that my system has serious defects. I have from time to time rectified some glaring deficiencies, but have decided that nothing but a radical change can make my plumbing beyond reproach."

Like many animal lovers, Sarah was very fond of her dog. "My dear little dog Snip has been ailing for a few days and today has seemed really very ill and it has distracted my attention from everything else."

Sarah had not traveled much in her adopted state of California. "I cannot say much about California as a state, as I have not seen much of it outside of the valley. I am not very enterprising as a traveler or sight seer [sic]. Every day I look up and see Lick Observatory glistening up on the top of Mt. Hamilton but I doubt if I ever get any nearer to it."

Sarah seems often to be dealing with construction issues. "I am constantly having to make an upheaval for some reason. For instance, my upper hall which leads to the sleeping apartments was rendered so unexpectedly dark by a little addition, that after several people had missed their footing on the stairs, I decided that safety demanded something to be done, so over a year ago I took out a wall and put in a skylight; then I had to have plastering done and as that could not well be done in the heat, I had to wait

Sarah's dog. Courtesy, History San Jose

for cooler weather; then I became rather worn and tired out and dismissed all the workmen to take such rest as I might through the winter." (This supports the belief that construction was not continuous.)

Sarah's ill health had made her quite lethargic. "The first thing I do after dinner is to go to bed. Just think how stupid I am to go to my night's rest before dark. That is what I have been doing lately. I sincerely hope I shall soon feel more wide awake and develop more energy and enterprise." (Apparently at this time she was not able to stay up until midnight to summon the spirits.)

These letters from Sarah to Jennie reveal the truly ordinary things that were important to Sarah and that took her attention and time.

CHAPTER 9

SARAH'S LEGACY

Sarah Winchester spent major parts of her adult life on two building projects. Both of these projects exist today, almost 100 years after her death. What has transpired with her mansion was completely unplanned, and I believe Sarah would be surprised today that it remains as part of her legacy. Her hospital, however, is the result of careful planning and was destined to be her legacy.

Sarah wanted to find a way to continue supporting the hospital well after her death. She accomplished this through her last will and testament. Rather than simply bequeathing money to her heirs, she set up trust funds for each of them. The recipients would receive interest on the trust fund during their lifetimes, but after their deaths the principal would go to support the hospital in Connecticut.[87]

Sarah in her carriage. Courtesy, History San Jose.

Sarah left trust funds to sixteen of her relatives. These included her sister, five nephews, four nieces, two great-nephews, and four great-nieces. Sarah's sister died before Sarah, so her share went to the sister's daughter, Marion Marriott. The amounts given to each ranged from $1,331,748 given to her niece Marion (which included her mother's share), to $26,635 given to her two great-nephews. The last of her heirs, her great-niece Anita McLean, passed away in 2010.

It is not known exactly how much the hospital received at the time of each heir's death or the fund's worth today, but it is surely substantial. Yale University no longer releases information about their donors including the amounts donated.

John Morthanos is a direct marketing consultant from Stratford, Connecticut. In 2001 he went to the Milford Hospital emergency room with what he thought was a heart attack. However, it was determined that he had not had a heart attack, and he was sent home. He became increasingly short of breath and dizzy but his primary physician told him not to worry about it. Over the next ten years, John consulted with many doctors. No doctor was able to diagnose what was causing his symptoms.

Eventually he was referred by a cardiologist to the Winchester Chest Clinic in New Haven. In 2011 they were finally able to correctly diagnose that John had

John Morthanos (bottom right) and staff of the Winchester Chest Clinic. Courtesy, John Morthanos.

idiopathic pulmonary fibrosis, a rare lung disease. They told John that he needed a lung transplant. The operation was successful and today John is doing well.

I contacted Mr. Morthanos and asked for his permission to include his story in this book. He replied:

> *"Bennett, I would be honoured. The team there [Winchester Chest Clinic] under Dr. Gulati saved my life."*[88]

Nearly a hundred years after Sarah's death, her mansion is still being appreciated by visitors and the clinic that she endowed is still saving lives.

These are the enduring legacies of Sarah Lockwood Winchester.

NOTES

1. Mary Jo Ignoffo, *Captive of the Labyrinth: Sarah L. Winchester, Heiress to the Rifle Fortune*, Columbia, MO: University of Missouri Press, 2010.

2. *New Haven City Directory*, New Haven, CT: Price, Lee & Co., 1882-1884.

3. *The General Hospital Society of Connecticut vs Francis A. Palloti, Attorney General*. Connecticut Superior Court, New Haven County, August 13, 1945, No. 66091.

4. Weldon Melick, "Sevenscore Gables," *Holiday*, February 1947. [Mary Jo Ignoffo, *Captive of the Labyrinth*.]

5. Ibid.

6. Lee A. and Susan Silva, "Winchester Won the West and Also Made the Winchester Mystery House Possible," *Wild West*, December 2001.

7. Richard Battin, "At Home with Sarah Winchester," *San Francisco Chronicle*, June 3, 1973.

8. Carl Hansen to Bertha Cramer, February 7, 1957, Hansen Collection, History San Jose.

9. Canceled check, March 8, 1917, Leib Collection, History San Jose.

10. *Holiday*, February 1947.

11. U.S. Census, San Mateo County, California, 1910.

12. Sarah Winchester to Frank Leib, November 8, 1906, Leib Collection, Stanford University Archives. [Mary Jo Ignoffo, *Captive of the Labyrinth*.]

13. Ibid.

14. Superior Court of California, Santa Clara County, Probate Case No. 12772, Sarah L. Winchester, inventory and appraisement.

15. *New Haven Hospital Eighty-Second Annual Report 1908*. New Haven, CT: New Haven Hospital, 1909.

16. Ibid.

17. *The General Hospital Society of Connecticut vs Francis A. Palloti,*

Attorney General

18. Ibid.

19. Ibid.

20. Charles Wayland to George Blumer, March 3, 1916, School of Medicine, Yale University, Records of the Dean, Yale University Archives.

21. *General Hospital Society of Connecticut Centenary, 1826-1926.* New Haven, CT: Tuttle, Morehouse & Taylor, 1926.

22. "New War Hospital in Allingtown is About Ready to Receive Patients," *New Haven Register*, March 17, 1918.

23. Charles Wayland to George Blumer, January 26, 1918, School of Medicine, Yale University, Records of the Dean, Yale University Archives.

24. Ibid.

25. George Blumer to Sarah Winchester, April 13, 1918, School of Medicine, Yale University, Records of the Dean, Yale University Archives.

26. Western Union telegram, Charles Wayland to George Blumer, February 1, 1918, School of Medicine, Yale University, Records of the Dean, Yale University Archives.

27. *History and Roster of the United States Army General Hospital No. 16.* New Haven, CT: Yale University Press, 1919.

28. William Wirt Winchester Hospital Brochure. New Haven, CT: New Haven Hospital, undated.

29. "Obituary," *New Haven Journal-Courier*, July 3, 1933.

30. Happyland Camp schedule, 1931, Medical History Library, Yale University.

31. U.S Centers for Disease Control, "Leading Causes of Death, 1900-1988," www.*cdc.gov/nchs/data/dvs/lead1900_98.pdf*, retrieved July 17, 2018.

32. *Grace-New Haven Community Hospital Annual Report, 1947-1949.* New Haven CT: Grace-New Haven Community Hospital, 1950.

33. *Grace-New Haven Community Hospital Annual Report, 1956-1958.* New Haven CT: Grace-New Haven Community Hospital, 1959.

34. California State Board of Health, Bureau of Vital Statistics, "Death

certificate of Sarah Winchester," 1922.

35. "A Woman Who Thinks She Will Die When Her House is Built," *San Jose Evening News*, March 29, 1895. [Mary Jo Ignoffo, *Captive of the Labyrinth*.]

36. "Superstition in Building," *American Architect and Building News*, February 8, 1896.

37. "Sarah Winchester is Summoned by Death," *San Jose Mercury*, September 7, 1922.

38. *Last Will and Testament of Sarah L. Winchester*, March 23, 1920, Garner Collection, History San Jose.

39. U.S. Patent Office, John H. Brown, of Rankin, Pennsylvania "Pleasure-Railway." Patent No. 762,022, June 7, 1904.

40. "Big Estate to be Amusement Park," *Palo Alto Times*, May 21, 1923.

41. Ruth Amet, "Mystery Novel Atmosphere Dominates Web of Rooms," *San Jose Mercury*, May 27, 1923. [Mary Jo Ignoffo, *Captive of the Labyrinth*.]

42. San Jose Convention & Visitors Bureau "Attractions and Amusement," www.sanjose.org/things-to-do/attractions-and-amusement, retrieved September 25, 2018.

43. Scott Bailey to Anne Garner, October 29, 1979, Garner Collection, History San Jose,

44. Ralph Rambo, *Lady of Mystery*. San Jose CA: Rosicrucian Press, 1967.

45. Mary Jo Ignoffo, *Captive of the Labyrinth*.

46. Jack Osler, "Mystery House," *Dayton* (Ohio) *Daily News*, January 18, 1976.

47. Carl Hansen to Bertha Cramer, February 7, 1957.

48. Bruce Spoon, *Sarah Winchester and Her House, How a Legend Grows*, Master's Thesis, San Jose State University, 1951.

49. "Mrs. Winchester was Sane Woman," *San Jose Mercury*, August 5, 1925. [Mary Jo Ignoffo, *Captive of the Labyrinth*.]

50. Michele and Tom Grimm, "Mysteries Highlight Visit to San Jose," *Los Angeles Times*, November 12, 1989.

51. *Holiday*, February 1947.

52. Ibid.

53. Bruce Spoon, *Sarah Winchester and Her House, How a Legend Grows*.

54. Ralph Rambo, *Lady of Mystery*.

55. *Wild West*, December 2001.

56. Donald Robesky to Anne Garner, June 25, 1979. Garner Collection, History San Jose.

57. "James Perkins Takes Own Life; Helped Build Winchester House," *San Jose Mercury*, January 19, 1948. [Mary Jo Ignoffo, *Captive of the Labyrinth*.]

58. William Orville Calhoun, "The Mystery House of San Jose," Sikeston (Missouri) Standard, July 14, 1933.

59. Donald Robesky to Anne Garner, June 25, 1979.

60. Ralph Rambo. *Lady of Mystery*.

61. Redmond Payne to Sarah Winchester, undated, Leib Collection, History San Jose.

62. John L. Von Blon, "Spirit House – World's Largest Home – is Open," *Dearborn* (Michigan) *Independent*, December 29, 1923.

63. *Holiday*, February 1947.

64. Ralph Rambo. *Lady of Mystery*.

65. Gerry O'Hara, "Sarah's Mansion: Winchester Mystery House," *California Camper*, October 1978.

66. Bruce Spoon. *Sarah Winchester and Her House, How a Legend Grows*.

67. Henry Calloway, "Taking the Mystery Out of the Mystery House," *Trailblazer*, August 1983. [Mary Jo Ignoffo, *Captive of the Labyrinth*.]

68. "Mrs. Winchester's Extraordinary Spook Palace," *American Weekly*, April 1, 1928.

69. Ibid.

70. Ralph Rambo. *Lady of Mystery*.

71. Kara Warner, "The Winchester Mansion: America's Most Haunted

House?" *People Magazine,* February 12, 2018.

72. *Connecticut Probate Court, New Haven District, New Haven Probate Records,* vol. 167, p.185, LDS microfilm #1405965.

73. Dean Jennings, "The House That Tragedy Built," *Coronet Magazine,* May 1945. [Mary Jo Ignoffo, *Captive of the Labyrinth.*]

74. *San Jose Mercury,* August 5, 1925. [Mary Jo Ignoffo, *Captive of the Labyrinth.*]

75. Carl Hansen to Bertha Cramer, February 7, 1957.

76. Ted Hansen to Helen Arbuckle, May 10, 1972, Arbuckle Collection, Stocklmeir Library and Archives, California History Center, De Anza College.

77. *Trailblazer,* August 1983.

78. Interview of Minnie Hall by Helen Arbuckle, February 20, 1979, Arbuckle Collection, Stocklmeir Library and Archives, California History Center, De Anza College.

79. Esther Talbot, "Sarah Winchester," *Rosicrucian Digest,* July 1975.

80. Receipt, February 27, 1914, Leib Collection, History San Jose.

81. *San Jose Mercury,* September 7, 1922.

82. *Holiday,* February 1947.

83. Ralph Rambo. *Lady of Mystery.*

84. Frank Bonanno, "Winchester Workman Says Famed Home's Owner Not Eccentric," *San Jose Evening News,* September 2, 1946.

85. *Trailblazer,* August 1983.

86. Sarah Winchester to Jennie Bennett, May 14, 1898, and June 11, 1898, Bennett-Winchester Family Papers, 1866-1977, Connecticut Historical Society.

87. *Last Will and Testament of Sarah L. Winchester,* March 23, 1920.

88. John Morthanos to the author, August 30, 2018.

BIBLIOGRAPHY

Archives

Primary sources were researched at the following archives and museums:

California Room, San Jose Public Library, San Jose, California

Connecticut Historical Society, Hartford, Connecticut.

History San Jose Archives, San Jose, California

Local History Room, New Haven Public Library, New Haven, Connecticut

Medical History Library, Harvey Cushing/John Hay Whitney Medical Library, Yale University, New Haven, Connecticut

San Mateo County History Museum, Redwood City, California

Stanford University Archives, Stanford, California

Stocklmeir Library and Archives, California History Center, De Anza College, Cupertino, California

Whitney Library, New Haven Museum, New Haven, Connecticut

Yale New Haven Hospital Archives, New Haven, Connecticut

Yale University Archives, New Haven, Connecticut

Sources

"$4,000,000 Left to Charity by Recluse Widow." *San Francisco Chronicle*, October 7, 1922.

Amet, Ruth. "Mystery Novel Atmosphere Dominates Web of Rooms." *San Jose Mercury*, May 27, 1923.

Anderson, Cynthia. *The Winchester Mystery House*. San Jose, CA: The Winchester Mystery House, 1997.

Arbuckle, Clyde and Roscoe D. Wyatt. *Historic Names, Persons and Places in Santa Clara County*. San Jose, CA: California Pioneers of Santa Clara County, 1948.

Bachko, Kitia. "A Terrified Woman, a Haunted House, and the Mystery of One of America's Most Famous Ghost Stories." *Scholastic Scope*, October 31, 2011.

Barnacle, Betty. "Obituary of William Pfeffer." *San Jose Mercury*, September 5, 2000.

Battin, Richard. "At Home with Sarah Winchester." *San Francisco Chronicle*, June 3, 1973.

Beronius, George. "Where Fact is Stranger than Fiction." *Los Angeles Times*, May 22, 1977.

"Big Estate to be Amusement Park." *Palo Alto* (California) *Times*, May 21, 1923.

Bonanno, Frank. "Winchester Workman Says Famed Home's Owner Not Eccentric." *San Jose Evening News*, September 2, 1946.

Brew, Tom. "Sarah Winchester Was No Ghost Buster." *San Jose Mercury*, October 31, 1984.

Brown, Edna May. *The Winchester Mystery House*. [publisher and date unknown]

Burness, Tad. *The Vintage House Book: Classic American Homes 1880-1980*. Iola, WI: Krause Publications, 2003.

Burrow, Gerald N. *A History of Yale's School of Medicine: Passing Torches to Others*. New Haven, CT: Yale University Press, 2002.

Byrnes, Robert. "V A Will Buy Hospital in New Haven." *Hartford* (Connecticut) *Courant*, February 27, 1946.

Calhoun, William Orville. "The Mystery House of San Jose." *Sikeston* (Missouri) *Standard*, July 14, 1933.

Calloway, Henry. "Taking the Mystery out of the Mystery House." *Trailblazer*, August 1983.

"Camp Happyland Opens for Season at Allingtown." *New Haven* (Connecticut) *Journal Courier*, July 3, 1933.

Cartmell, Robert. *The Incredible Scream Machine: A History of the Roller Coaster*. Fairview Park, OH: Amusement Park Books, 1987.

Christian, Eugene. *Little Lessons in Corrective Eating*. New York: Corrective Eating Society, Inc., 1916.

Connecticut General Assembly. *Report of Special Commission Appointed to Investigate Tuberculosis*. Hartford, CT: State of Connecticut, 1908.

Corbett, Leslie Ayn. *The Winchester Mystery House*. [unpublished] 1982. viewed in California Room, San Jose Public Library.

"Court Confirms Winchester Sale: Famous Place Becomes Property of Four Local Businessmen." *San Jose Mercury*, December 16, 1922.

Creffield, Charlene. "Why Sarah Winchester Kept on Building." *San Jose Mercury*, November 14, 1984.

Custer, Joe. "Mystery Shrouds One-Time Famous Spirit Haven." *San Bernardino County* (California) *Sun*, May 17, 1936.

Daley, Edith. "Old House at Winchester Place Gives up some of its Well Guarded Secrets." (serial in seven installments) *San Jose Evening News*, September 18-25, 1922.

Dickey, Colin. *Ghostland: An American History in Haunted Places*. New York: Penguin Books, 2016.

"An Eerie World: The Winchester House." *San Francisco Chronicle*, December 11, 1949.

Faltersack, Fred P. "The Strangest House in the World." *Wide World Magazine*, March 1929.

Federal Writers' Project. *California: A Guide to the Golden State*. New York: Hastings House, 1939.

Ferut, Michael. *Winchester Mystery House*. Minneapolis, MN: Bellwether Media, 2015.

"Fifty Percent of Quota is Subscribed." *San Jose Mercury*, May 7, 1919.

Frey, Christine. *Sarah Pardee Winchester: The Supposed "Lady of Mystery."* [unpublished] 1996. viewed in California Room, San Jose Public Library.

General Hospital Society of Connecticut Centenary, 1826-1926. New Haven, CT: Tuttle, Morehouse & Taylor, 1926.

Gittings, Catherine. "The Lady and the Ark." *Sunset Magazine*, November 2, 1916.

Grant, Joanne. "Another Side to Enigmatic Winchester." *San Jose Mercury*, May 11, 1992.

Gray, Merle H. "The Workshop of a Woman Architect." *San Jose Evening News,* July 16, 1911.

Grimm, Michele and Tom Grimm. "Mysteries Highlight Visit to San Jose." *Los Angeles Times*, November 12, 1989.

Haag, Pamela. *Gunning of America: Business and the Making of American Gun Culture*. New York: Basic Books, 2016.

Harder, Nick. "Remodeling Lessons from the Famous." *Marysville* (California) *Appeal-Democrat*, July 22, 2000.

Hawkins, Joseph A. "Taking Mystery out of the Mystery House." *New Haven* (Connecticut) *Register*, January 7, 1940.

Heritage of Connecticut's First Hospital. New Haven, CT: Yale-New Haven Hospital, 1976.

Hess, Alan. "Sarah Winchester Deserves Recognition." *San Jose Mercury*, February 15, 1987.

Hicks, Tony. "Winchester House Still a Total Mystery." *San Jose Mercury*, October 19, 2014.

Hillinger, Charles. "Spirits Move Sarah to Build and Build." *Los Angeles Times*, September 8, 1974.

History and Roster of the United States Army General Hospital No. 16. New Haven, CT: Yale University Press, 1929.

Hosley, William N. *Colt: The Making of an American Legend*. Amherst, MA: University of Massachusetts Press, 1996.

"Hospital Gets Fund in Winchester Will." *San Jose Mercury*, October 7, 1922.

Hotchkiss, Fanny Winchester. *Winchester Notes*. New Haven, CT: Tuttle, Morehouse & Taylor, 1912.

"Houdini Bent on Exposing Tricks of Spiritualism." *Oregon Daily Journal*, November 3, 1924.

"House for Homeless Ghosts?" *Austin* (Texas) *American-Statesman*, November 9, 1924.

"The House That Just Grew." *Reader's Digest,* August 1938.

"Houzz TV: Beyond the Ghost Stories of the Winchester Mystery House." Online video clip. Houzz, [date unknown] Web. Accessed October 11, 2018.

Ignoffo, Mary Jo. *Captive of the Labyrinth: Sarah L. Winchester, Heiress to the Rifle Fortune*. Columbia, MO: University of Missouri Press, 2010.

Ikonian, Therese. "Books Give Way to People Who Speak from Memory." *San Jose Mercury*, March 27, 1985.

James Perkins Takes Own Life; Helped Build Winchester House." *San Jose Mercury*, January 9, 1948.

Jankowiak-Hirsch, Rose Ann. *Crystal Memories: 101 Years of Fun at Crystal Beach Park*. Palmyra, NY: R.A. Jankowiak-Hirsch, 2004.

Jennings, Dean. "The House That Tragedy Built." *Coronet*, May 1945.

Johnston, Ellen W. "Sarah Winchester: Fiction Stranger Than Truth." *Heritage West*, March 1983.

Junker, Christine R. "Unruly Women and Their Crazy Houses." *Home Cultures*, September 2015.

Kae, William E. *Crystal Beach Park: A Century of Screams*. Buffalo, NY: Cyclone Books, 2011.

Kaufman, Marion B. "Our County Heritage." *San Jose Mercury*, March 28, 1965.

"Kind Hearts -- Good Deeds." *Los Angeles Times*, December 9, 1909.

"Landmark House Sarah's 'Jack' Built." *San Jose Mercury*, April 26, 1974.

"Living in an Ark." *San Mateo (California) Times*, August 6, 1904.

Majd, Nilufar. *Sarah Winchester and Her House of Mystery*. [unpublished] 1998. viewed in California Room, San Jose Public Library.

"Manager of Winchester Place Called by Death." *San Jose Evening Mercury*, October 26, 1909

Mars, Amaury. *Reminiscences of the Santa Clara Valley and San Jose*. San Francisco, CA: Artistic Publishers, 1901.

Matson, Susan. *The Legend of Sarah Winchester and Her Home*. [unpublished] 1982. viewed in California Room, San Jose Public Library.

"May Remove." *San Jose Mercury*, April 1, 1903.

May, Antoinette. "Sarah Kept On Building to Quiet the Ghosts." *Sacramento* (California) *Union*, October 31, 1975.

Melick, Weldon. "Sevenscore Gables." *Holiday*, February 1947.

"The Moulton Place at Fair Oaks." *Redwood City* (California) *Democrat*, October 8, 1903.

"Mrs. S. Winchester Claimed by Death." *Palo Alto* (California) *Times*, September 7, 1922.

"Mrs. Winchester Not Ill; Branded Fake." *San Jose Mercury*, June 11, 1911.

"Mrs. Winchester Was Sane Woman." *San Jose Mercury*, August 5, 1925.

"Mrs. Winchester was Sane, Guide States." *San Jose Evening News*, September 10, 1946.

"Mrs. Winchester's Extraordinary Spook Palace." *American Weekly*, April 1, 1928.

"Mystery Man Kidnapped to Save His Life." *San Francisco Examiner*, August 13, 1915.

New Haven City Directory. New Haven, CT: Price & Lee, 1882-84.

"New War Hospital in Allingtown is About Ready to Receive Patients." *New Haven* (Connecticut) *Register*, March 17, 1918.

Newfarmer, Trish. "The Winchester House (1985)." Online video clip. YouTube. History San Jose, September 11, 2017. Web. Accessed October 11, 2018.

Nickell, Joe. "Winchester Mystery House: Fact vs Fancy." *Skeptical Inquirer*, September 2002.

"Obituary." *New Haven* (Connecticut) *Journal Courier*, September 8, 1922.

O'Hara, Gerry. "Sarah's Mansion: Winchester Mystery House." *California Camper*, October 1978.

"Old and New Houses." *San Francisco Chronicle*, June 19, 1887.

Omstead, Lorena Ann. "House That Spirits Built." *National Motorist*, July 1946.

"One of the Hayes Nominees Strongly Rebuked by Woman." *San Jose Evening News*, November 1, 1902.

"Only Gossip, No Truth in the Story of the Winchester Place." *San Jose Evening News*, October 11, 1897.

Osler, Jack. "Mystery House." *Dayton* (Ohio) *Daily News*, January 18, 1976.

O'Toole, Thomas. "Wine and Mystery in Old San Jose." *Willoughby* (Ohio) *News-Herald*, March 23, 1975.

Page, Barbara. "A Night in the Mystery House." *Campbell* (California) *Press*, August 20, 1975.

Paltz, Kendra K. *Toward an Ethical Representation of Sarah Winchester*. (Master's Thesis) Normal, IL: Illinois State University, 2011.

Pendergast, William. "The Woman Who Lived Alone in a Home with 160 Rooms." *New Haven* (Connecticut) *Register*, June 7, 1964.

Pierce, Marjorie. "She Played Musical Homes." *San Jose Mercury*, July 22, 1973.

Pitts, William. "Grieving Widow Hides Self There Until Her Death." *Port Huron* (Michigan) *Times Herald*, June 19, 1923.

Rambo, Ralph. *Almost Forgotten: Cartoon Pen and Inklings of the Old Santa Clara Valley*. San Jose, CA: [publisher unknown], 1964.

Rambo, Ralph. *Lady of Mystery*. San Jose, CA: Rosicrucian Press, 1967.

Rambo, Ralph. *Remember When: A Boy's-Eye View of an Old Valley*. San Jose, CA: Rosicrucian Press, 1965.

Rambo, Ralph. "Applause for *Extra* Story on Winchester Mystery House." *San Jose Mercury*, November 14, 1984.

Reese, Lucas. *Making Money with Myth: The Winchester Mystery House, 1922-2002*. [unpublished] 2003. viewed in California Room, San Jose Public Library.

Rio, Delia. "Sarah Winchester Goes on Trial." *San Jose Mercury*, April 1, 1989.

Robbins, Millie. "The Mysterious Mrs. Winchester." *San Francisco Chronicle*, November 21, 1969.

Robbins, Millie. "The Mystery House Puzzle." *San Francisco Chronicle*, June 19, 1966.

Rossi, Erno. *Crystal Beach: The Good Old Days*. Port Colborne, Ontario, Canada: Seventy Seven Publishing, 2005.

"Sarah Winchester Dies at San Jose." *Oakland* (California) *Tribune*, September 7, 1922.

"Sarah Winchester is Summoned by Death." *San Jose Mercury*, September 7, 1922.

"Sarah Winchester was Quite Rich." *Mansfield* (Ohio) *News-Journal*, July 29, 1984.

Schultz, Judi. "Journey with Judi: House of Mystery." *San Jose Mercury*, September 14, 1970.

Selby, Lisa L. *The Inscrutable Mrs. Winchester*. Baltimore, MD: PublishAmerica, 2006.

"Sells Her Mansion and Defies Spirits." *San Francisco Examiner*, November 8, 1911.

Silva, Lee A. and Susan Silva. "Winchester Won the West and Also Made the Winchester Mystery House Possible." *Wild West*, December 2001.

"SJ Mystery House Manager's Rites Set for Tomorrow." *San Jose Mercury*, June 11, 1945.

Smith, Karen. "Built to be Haunted." *Palo Alto* (California) *Peninsula Times-Tribune*, October 27, 1988.

Smith, Rebecca. "Colleagues Remember Promoter of Winchester Mystery House." *San Jose Mercury*, February 9, 1997.

Smith, Susy. *Prominent American Ghosts*. New York: Dell, 1967.

"Spirit Message on Winchester Place Received." *San Jose Evening News*, November 29, 1922.

"Spiritualism -- Is It of God, Man, or the Devil?" *Bakersfield Californian*, February 11, 1933.

Spoon, Bruce. *Sarah Winchester and Her House: How a Legend Grows*. (Master's Thesis) San Jose, CA: San Jose State University, 1951.

Stannard, Ed. "Connecticut's Own Learn Getting the Right Diagnosis Takes Effort, Patience." *New Haven* (Connecticut) *Register*, October 6, 2013.

Stark, John. "Sarah Winchester's Ghostly Penance." *San Francisco Examiner*, August 29, 1976.

"State to Note Two Landmarks." *San Jose Mercury*, January 8, 1974.

"Strangest Structure." *San Jose Evening News*, October 9, 1897.

"Superstition in Building." *American Architect and Building News*, February 8, 1896.

Svanevik, Michael. "Sarah L. Winchester: Deranged or Defamed?" *San Mateo* (California) *Times*, January 30, 1987.

Talbot, Esther. "Sarah Winchester." *Rosicrucian Digest*, July 1975.

Thorndike, Joseph J. Jr. *Magnificent Builders and Their Dream Houses*. London, England: Elek, 1978.

Trevelyan, Laura. *Winchester: The Gun That Built an American Dynasty*. New Haven, CT: Yale University Press, 2016.

"The 'Truth' About Sarah Winchester." *San Jose Mercury*, November 14, 1984.

Turner, Erin H. *More than Petticoats: Remarkable California Women*. Guilford, CT: Globe Pequot, 1999.

Tuttle, Gene. "Title Search Uncovers Strange Facts." *San Jose Mercury*, April 14, 1979.

"A Visit to a Mystery House." *Oakland* (California) *Tribune*, August 9, 1953.

Von Blon, John L. "Spirit House -- World's Largest Home -- Is Open." *Dearborn* (Michigan) *Independent*, December 29, 1923.

Walker, Wayne. "Monument to Fear." *Elks Magazine*, June 1976.

Warner, Kara. "The Winchester Mansion: America's Most Haunted House?" *People Magazine*, February 12, 2018.

Watson, Jeanette. *Campbell, the Orchard City*. Campbell, CA: Campbell Historical Museum Association, 1989.

Weimers, Leigh. "Winchester Mystery Evoked in Fun Play." *San Jose Mercury*, September 14, 2005.

Williamson, Harold. *Winchester: The Gun That Won the West*. New York: Barnes, 1952.

"Winchester Estate Leased as Amusement Park for 10 Yrs." *San Jose Mercury*, May 20, 1923.

"Winchester Home is Opened as Resort." *Palo Alto* (California) *Times*, June 29, 1923.

"Winchester Home Sold; the House Upon Which Thousands Spent Held Almost Valueless." *San Jose Evening News*, December 1, 1922.

"Winchester House." *San Jose Mercury*, June 17, 1951.

"Winchester of Mystery House Fame Proves Real Mystery." *San Jose Mercury*, December 1, 1944.

"Winchester Will Filed." *San Jose Mercury*, September 14, 1922.

"Winchester Will Leave Millions to Charity." *Palo Alto* (California) *Times*, October 8, 1922.

"A Woman Who Thinks She Will Die When Her House is Built." *San Jose Evening News*, March 29, 1895.

Wouk, Henry. *Tuberculosis*. New York: Marshall Cavendish Benchmark, 2010.

Woulfl, Genevieve. *Sarah Pardee Winchester, A Driven Woman*. San Carlos, CA: Redwood Publishers, 1986.

Zyda, Joan. "Mystery Mansion is Built on Guilt." *Chicago Tribune*, July 14, 1976.

Printed in Great Britain
by Amazon